Beating the Bounds

of the parish of Affpuddle and Turnerspuddle

First published in Great Britain 2018
by Scene in Britain

Text copyright © Andrew Knox

Photographs copyright © Leonora Sheppard

Design and production by Roger Stayte

The author's moral rights have been asserted. All rights reserved. No part of this publication may be reproduced, stored in a retrieval system or transmitted in any form or by any means, electronic, mechanical, photocopying, recording or otherwise without the prior permission of the copyright owner.

A CIP record of this book is available from the British Library.

ISBN: 978 1 5272 1718 8

 © Crown Copyright 2018 Ordnance Survey 100059650

The contents of this book are believed to be correct at the time of publishing. The Publishers cannot be held responsible for any errors or omissions or for the consequences of any reliance on the information it provides. This does not affect your statutory rights.

Public rights of way shown on this map have been taken from Local Authority definitive maps. The representation on this map of any other road, track or path is no evidence of the existence of a right of way.

We have tried to ensure accuracy in this book, but things do change.

CONTENTS

Foreword	5
A brief history	6
Information	9
Overview map	12
The Walk	15
Circular Walk A	77
Circular Walk B	83
Circular Walk C	88
The Countryside Code	94

Foreword

Ten years ago I set out on a journey as a fledgling parish councillor. At the time I didn't know the twists and turns of the way ahead, the strangeness of the terrain, or what obstacles and challenges might lie in my path. As with all adventures, I encountered many interesting characters along the way and I have learnt much and made new friends.

To mark my tenth anniversary, and to look back over the decade, I decided to undertake a different sort of adventure. I settled on the idea of retracing the steps of an old annual ritual, marking the parish boundary called 'Beating the Bounds'. I considered this journey to represent a more personal connection between myself and our parish as well as presenting its own challenges, like finding the closest route to the parish boundary itself whilst keeping to public rights of way.

Thinking about how I might share my experience with my fellow councillors, I decided to prepare a short pamphlet. This idea was taken up by my husband Andrew who produced a handwritten account of the walk as a birthday present. Our friends, Leonora and Roger, then encouraged us to develop the idea a stage further, and with their considerable help this short book has been produced.

My wish is to share the walk and the wonderfully varied landscape of our parish with anyone who cares to accept the invitation to retrace this traditional 'circumambulation', either by foot or from the comfort of an armchair.

Sue Jones

Turnerspuddle 2018

A brief history

Dorset folklorist, John Symonds Udal wrote about the traditions of 'Beating the Bounds' on Holy Thursday or Ascension Day in Dorset.

Beating the Bounds

It was the general custom in olden days, and is still observed in many parishes in Dorsetshire, for certain persons to go round, or perambulate the boundaries or limits of their own particular parish in Rogation Week, or, - to be more precise, - on one of the three days before Holy Thursday or Ascension Day, though more often, I think, on Holy Thursday itself. Upon these occasions, as Brand tells us,

'the minister, accompanied by his churchwardens and parishioners, were wont to deprecate the vengeance of God, beg a blessing on the fruits of the earth, and preserve the rights and properties of the parish.'

In Dorsetshire the last of these objects would seem to be the one principally or solely considered at the present day. This perambulation is known as 'Beating the Bounds'.

Before I proceed to the 'perambulations' of particular parishes, I would like to produce in full the most amusing account of this interesting and useful custom contributed by William Barnes to Hone's Year Book as existing in Dorsetshire in his younger days. He says,

'A Perambulation, or, as it might be more correctly called, a circumambulation, is the custom of going round the boundaries of a manor or parish, with witnesses, to determine and preserve recollection of its extent, and to see that no encroachments have been made upon it, and that the landmarks have not been taken away.

It is a proceeding commonly regulated by the steward, who takes with him a few men and several boys who are required to particularly observe the boundaries traced out, and thereby qualify themselves for witnesses in the event of any dispute about the landmarks or extent of the manor at a future day.

Here is an extract from his book 'Dorsetshire Folk-lore' which was first published in 1922.

In order that they may not forget the lines and marks of separation they 'take pains' at almost every turning.

For instance, if the boundary be a stream, one of the boys is tossed into it; if a broad ditch, the boys are offered money to jump over it, in which they, of course, fail, and pitch into the mud, where they stick as firmly as if they had been rooted there for the season; if a hedge, a sapling is cut out of it and used in afflicting that part of their bodies upon which they rest in the posture between standing and lying; if a wall, they are to have a race on the top of it, when, in trying to pass each other, they fall over on each side, some descending, perhaps, into the still stygian waters of a ditch, and others thrusting the 'human face divine' into a bed of nettles; if the boundary be a sunny bank, they sit down upon it and get a treat of beer and bread and cheese, and, perhaps, a glass of spirits.

When these boys grow up to be men, if it happens that one of them should be asked if a particular stream were the boundary of the manor he had perambulated, he would be sure to say, in the manner of Sancho Panza, 'Ees, that 'tis, I'm sure o't, by the same token that I were tossed into't, and paddled about there lik' a water-rot till I wor hafe dead.'

If he should be asked whether the aforesaid pleasant bank were, a boundary: 'O, ees it be,' he would say, 'that's where we squat down and tucked in a skinvull of vittles and drink.'

With regard to any boundary perambulation after that he would most likely declare, 'I won't be sartin; I got zo muddled up top o' the banks, that don' know where we ambulated arter that.'

Information

Suggested maps	Ordnance Survey **Explorer OL15** (1: 25,000) Purbeck & South Dorset **Explorer 117** (1: 25,000) Cerne Abbas & Bere Regis
Distance	13 ⅓ miles
Duration	about 4 hours
Paths	gravel, stony, muddy, woodland and heathland
Dog friendly	yes, on a lead where necessary
Public toilets	none

Public footpaths across MOD land

To enjoy your walk please be warned of the following:

Do NOT touch or pick up ANY suspicious objects, they may cause injury or be fatal.

Keep to the footpath, designated by the yellow-topped posts, at all times.

There is NO public access along the tank tracks.

Stay alert when crossing tank tracks, vehicles may be quiet and travelling at speed.

No picnicking or stopping is allowed.

Dogs are to be kept on a short lead.

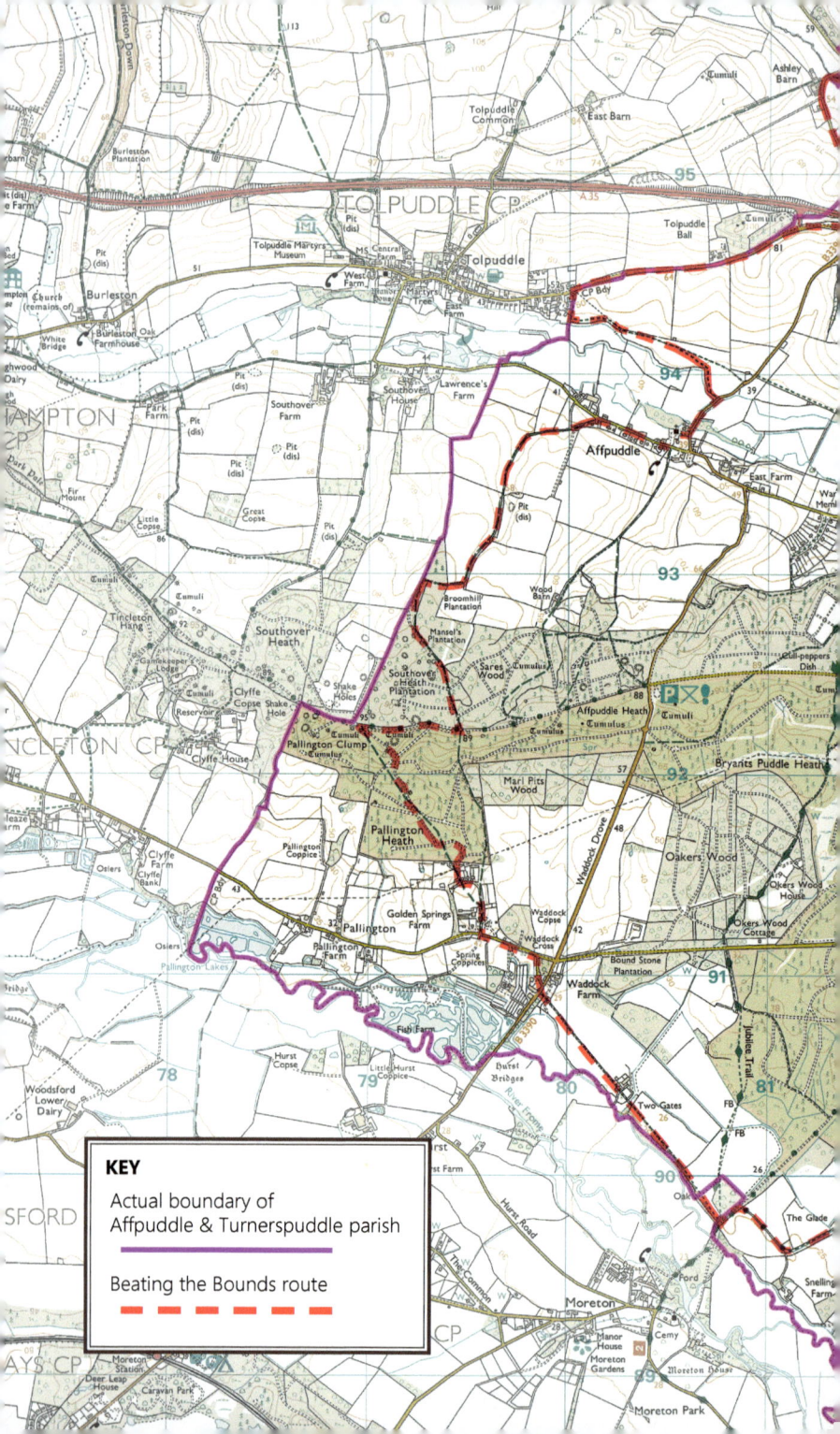

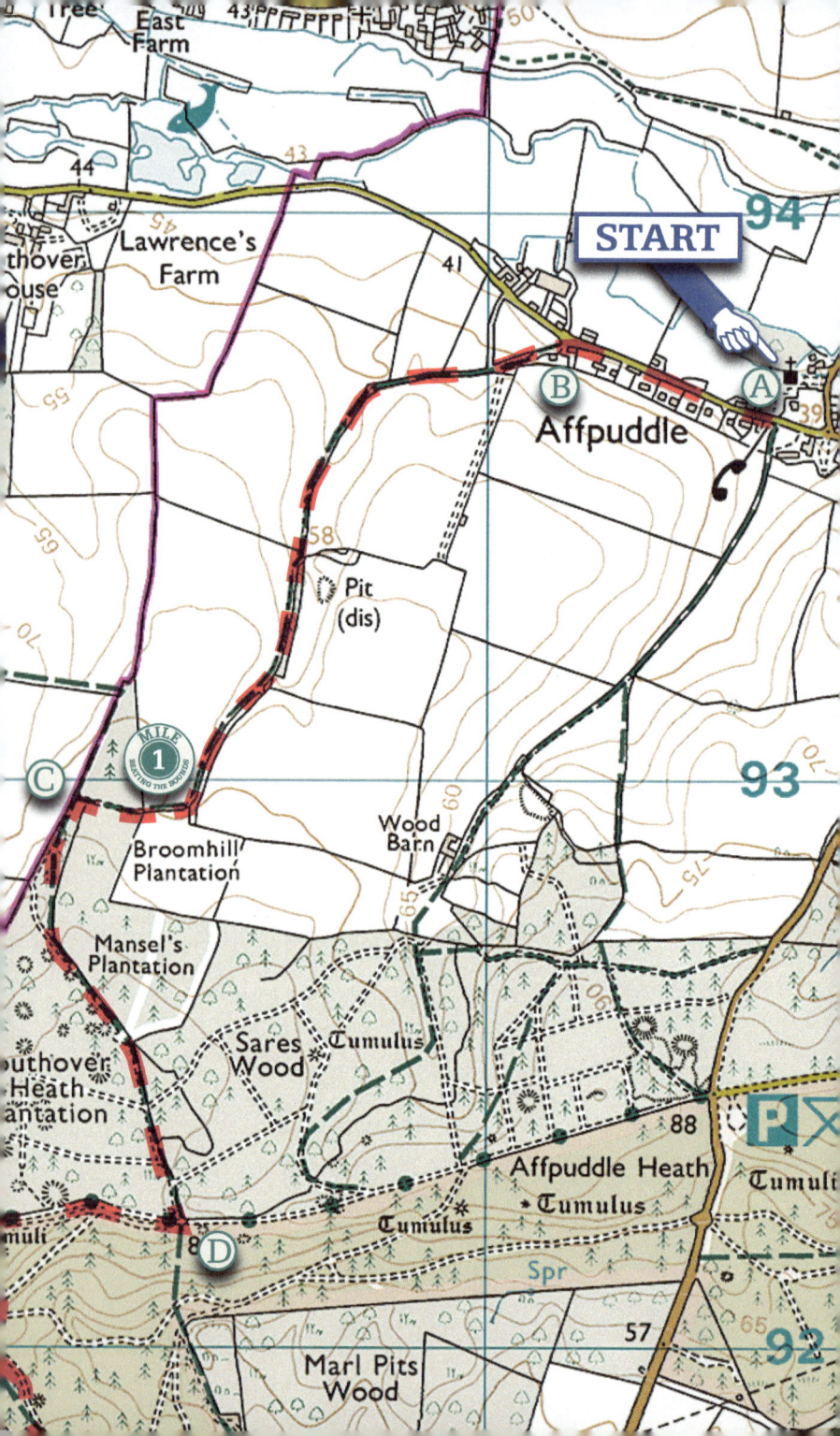

The Walk

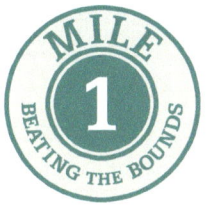

Start at the church of St. Laurence Affpuddle, where there is room enough for a few cars to park alongside the churchyard Ⓐ.

This fine church, which is open daily, dates originally from the 13th century, enlarged later in the 15th century with an aisle and a splendid tower in the Perpendicular style.

Inside are interesting pew ends, some with poppy head finials. The pulpit has five panels containing finely carved figures, below which are medallions with the symbols of the Four Evangelists and the fifth of the pelican (which, according to legend, would pierce its own chest in order to feed blood to its young).

Head west along the road through the village, and then where the road bears slightly right Ⓑ, take the bridleway on the left, initially a metalled track, leading up a slight incline.

Ignoring tracks to the left and right, continue along the bridleway between hedges and then curving left to skirt the edge of first one large field, and then a second, eventually reaching a gate by a large oak tree in front of a dark conifer wood.

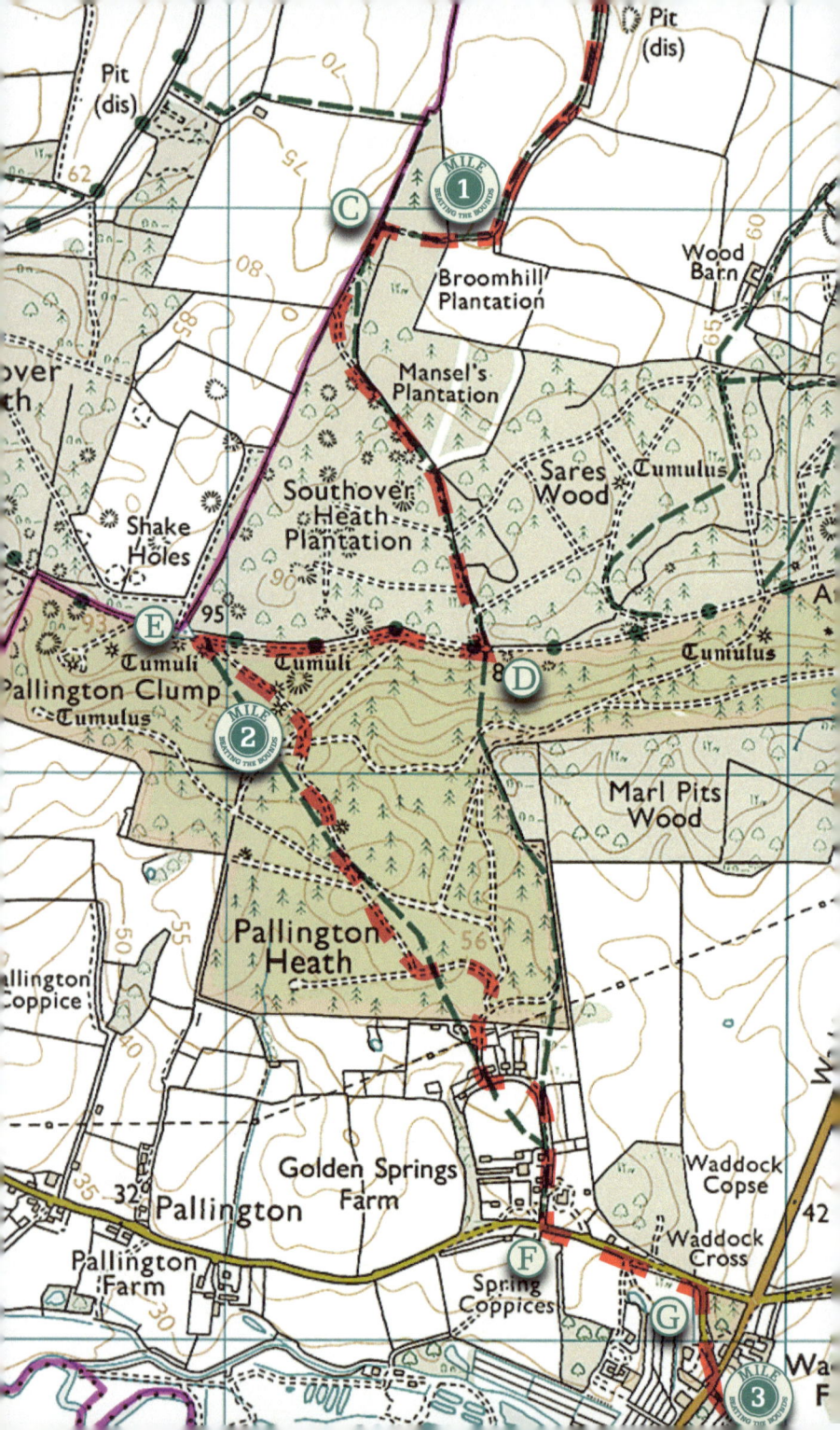

Passing through the gate, follow the path through the towering conifers. This section may be rutted and muddy in wet weather, but after a short distance the path meets another at right angles Ⓒ, and turning left the new path should be firmer underfoot. The woodland now becomes slightly more open, with oak and beech mixed in, and in springtime bluebells line the path.

Keep to the main track, ignoring any forestry tracks to the left or right, eventually passing to the side of a metal vehicle barrier to emerge onto a substantial track, the Hardy Way Ⓓ.

Turn right along this track, where now birch and sweet chestnut are included in the mix of trees on each side. After a short distance, a large hollow can be seen to the right, one of the natural sinkholes that can be seen in the area caused by subsidence in the chalk below the gravel subsoil (the most well-known being Culpeppers Dish in the central part of the parish).

Continue along the track, and where there is a clearing in the trees to the left, look out for a path doubling back at a sharp angle Ⓔ on the left hand side.

The path is waymarked with a blue arrow, although the waymark post is set back a few yards and could be easily missed.

The path is quite narrow, flanked on either side by bushy heather that will tickle your ankles.

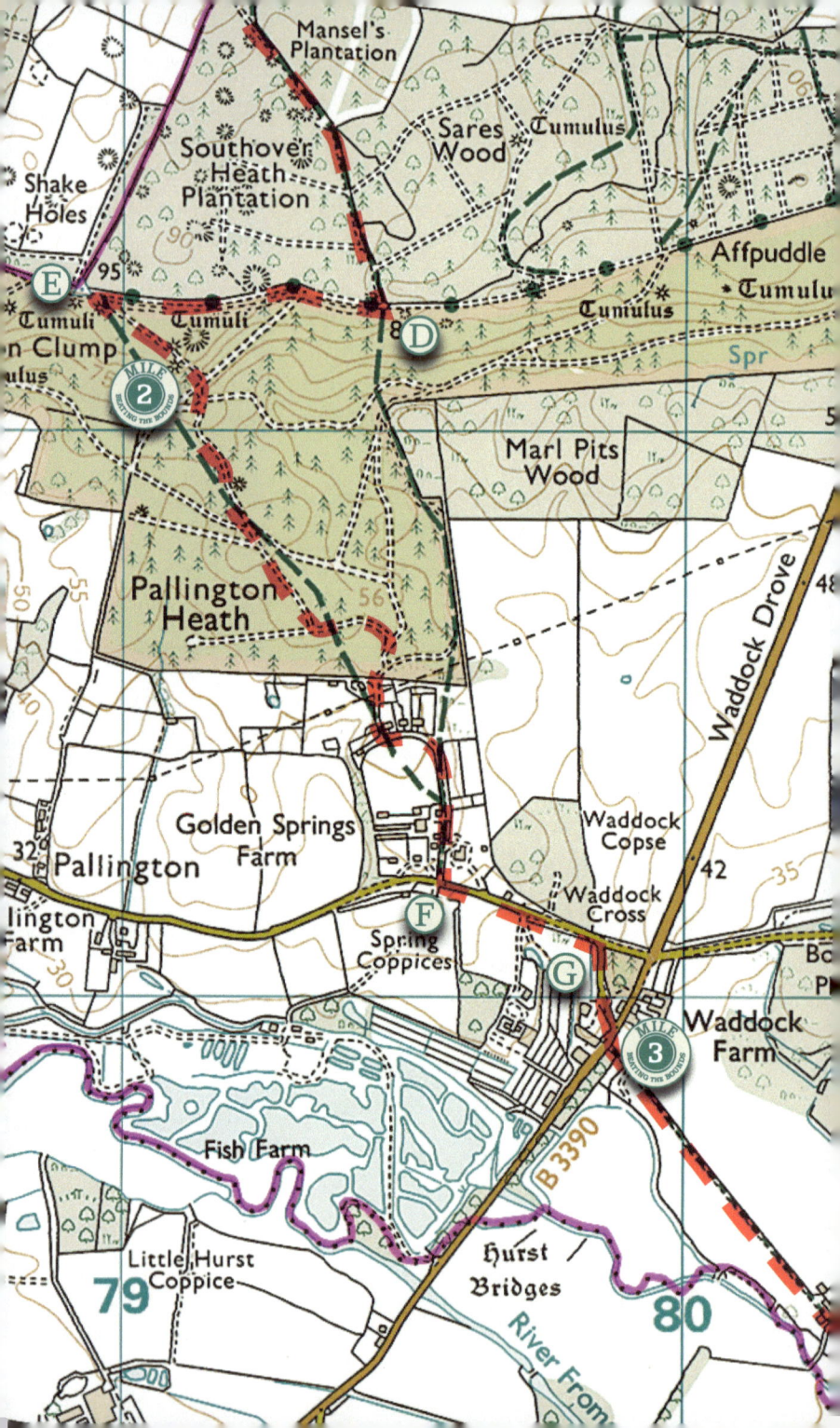

Just beyond a green painted bench on the right (placed no doubt to enjoy the views over Pallington, now unfortunately obscured by the rising conifers), the path descends steeply. At the bottom of the steepest section, cross over first one track at an angle, then shortly after cross another, and then a third, keeping straight ahead following the blue arrow waymark.

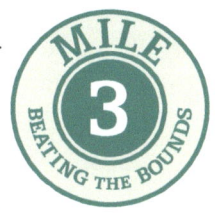

Bear left at a further blue arrow, and then swing right keeping to the main track as two other tracks come in from the left in quick succession. Pass under the pylon lines to emerge beyond a metal vehicle barrier onto an unmetalled lane giving access to a number of houses.

Turn left along this lane, which swings right to skirt a tree-lined paddock, then meeting a minor road Ⓕ at a point where there is a glimpse of the distant Purbeck hills. Turn left along this road, passing a post box and parish notice board, and then just before Waddock Cross, take the right-hand fork in the road, leading to the B3390 a short way ahead Ⓖ.

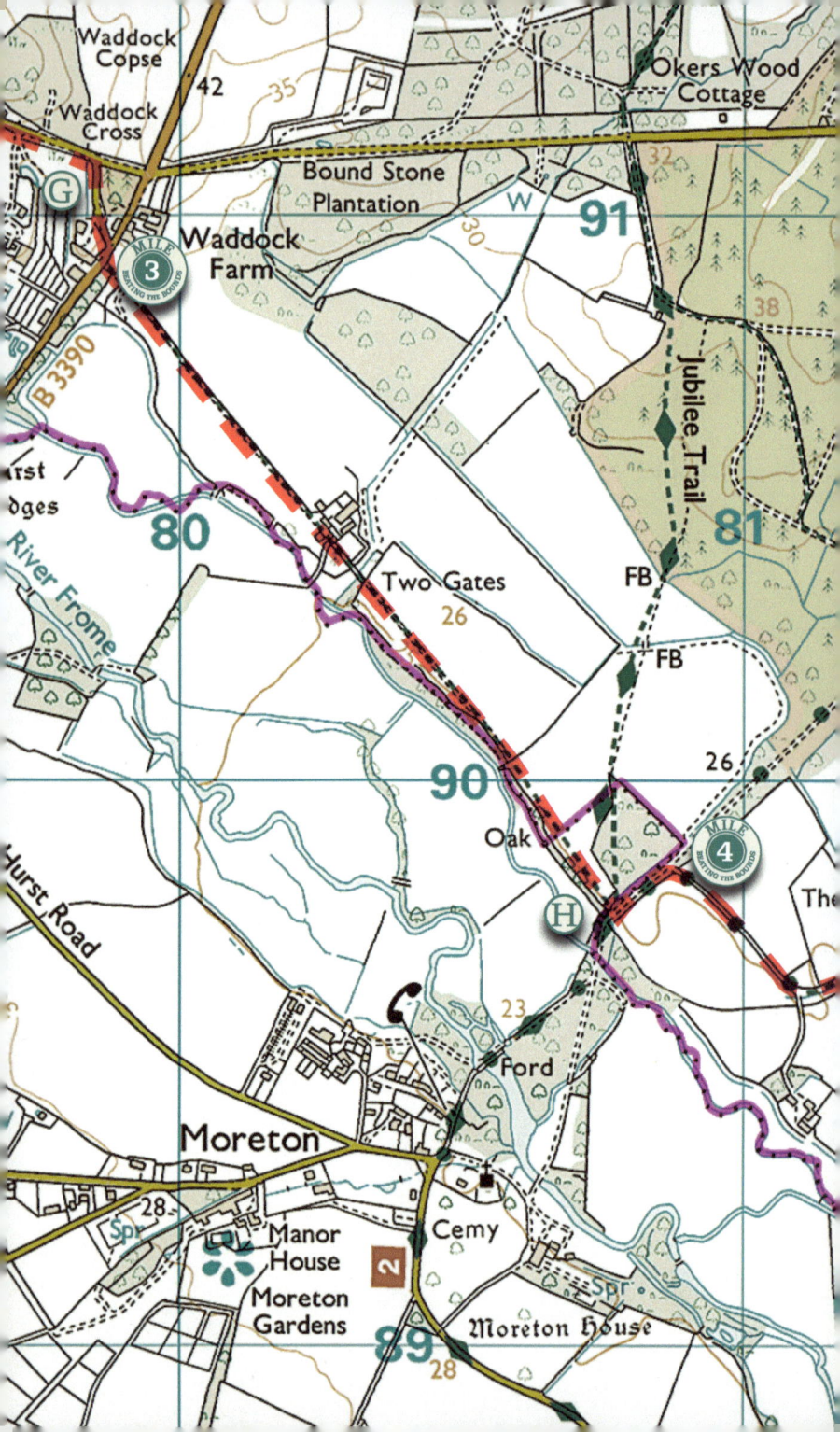

Cross the B3390, and after a few yards, opposite a pair of amorous metal figures, take the footpath signed to Waddock Dairy on the left. Cross the cattle grid and continue along the substantial track to the dairy, where at milking time you may have to wait patiently for a while as the cows amble slowly across into or out of the dairy (or find a way through the bovine traffic).

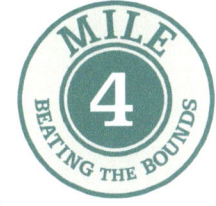

Beyond the dairy, the track continues straight ahead, becoming narrower, and then reducing to a grassy path, eventually coming to a wooden gate and stile leading onto the well-trodden track of Moreton Drive Ⓗ.

A short detour may be taken here to the right towards Moreton where there is a long, low footbridge and ford across a wide, shallow section of the River Frome. This is a popular spot for children in the summer months.

However, to continue Beating the Bounds, turn left along Moreton Drive, and after a short distance turn right along a track signed as the Lawrence Trail.

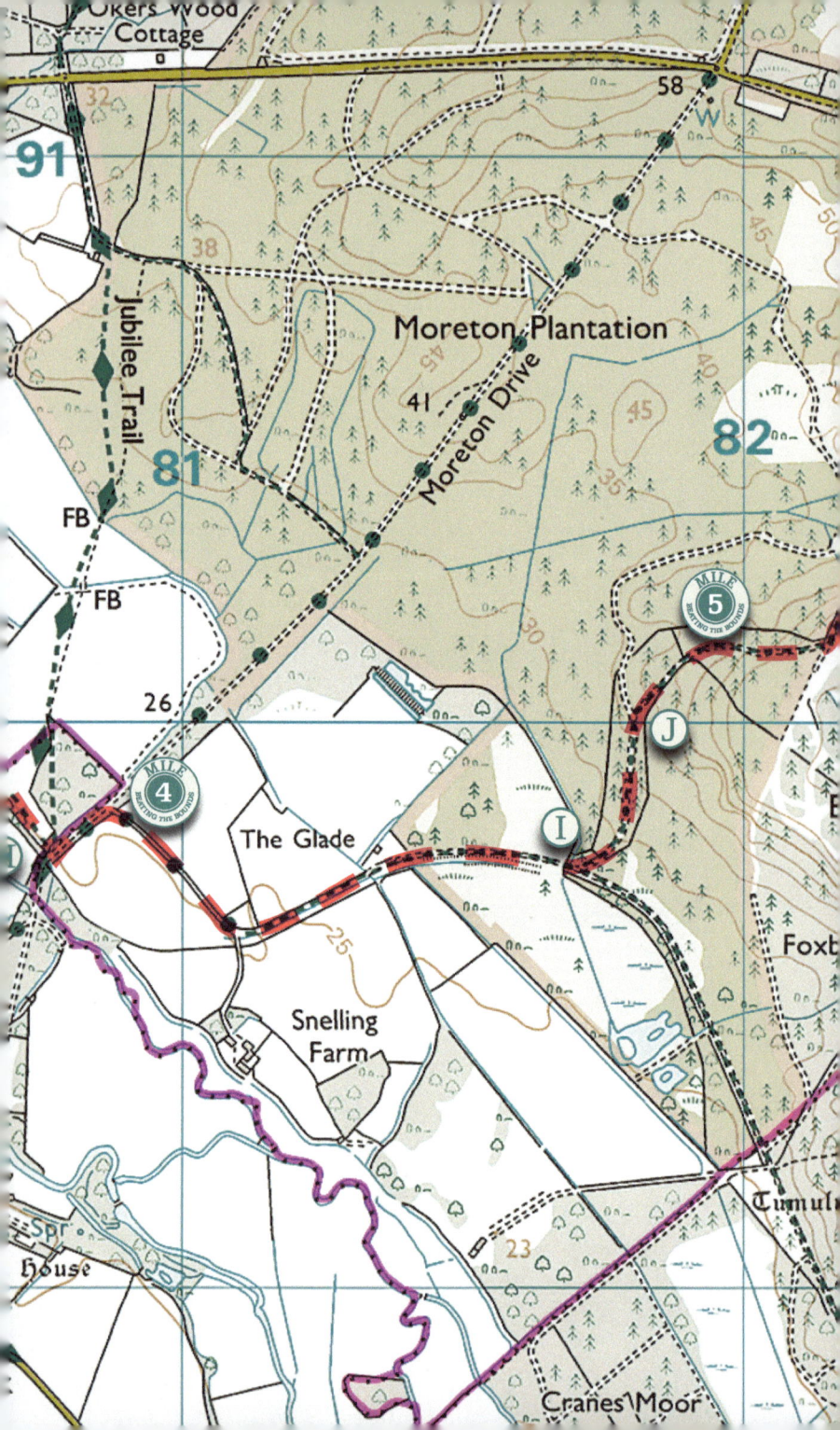

Pass to the left of a dying oak tree (with just two small branches valiantly clinging to life at the time of writing), and then swing to the left and continue through a pleasant section of mixed woodland. Pass a ruined house on the left and go through a wooden gate, after which the trees begin to thin until the path emerges into a Savanna-like grassland area.

At a junction of tracks by a group of young oaks Ⓘ, turn left keeping to the signed Lawrence Trail, and follow the sandy path flanked at first by bracken and gorse, and then by conifers.

A little way ahead, leave the main track, turning right onto a path opposite another Lawrence Trail waymark Ⓙ.

Head uphill, keeping to the stony path, until reaching a metal kissing gate in the fence marking the edge of the military training area. There is a sign indicating that your enjoyment of the walk depends on, amongst other things, NOT touching ANY suspicious objects, and keeping to the footpath designated by the yellow-topped posts at all times.

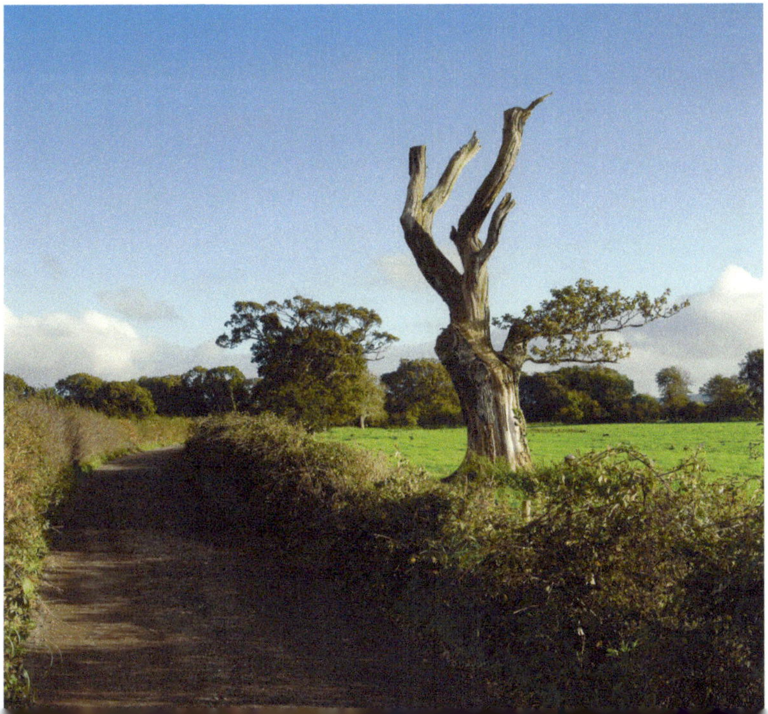

34

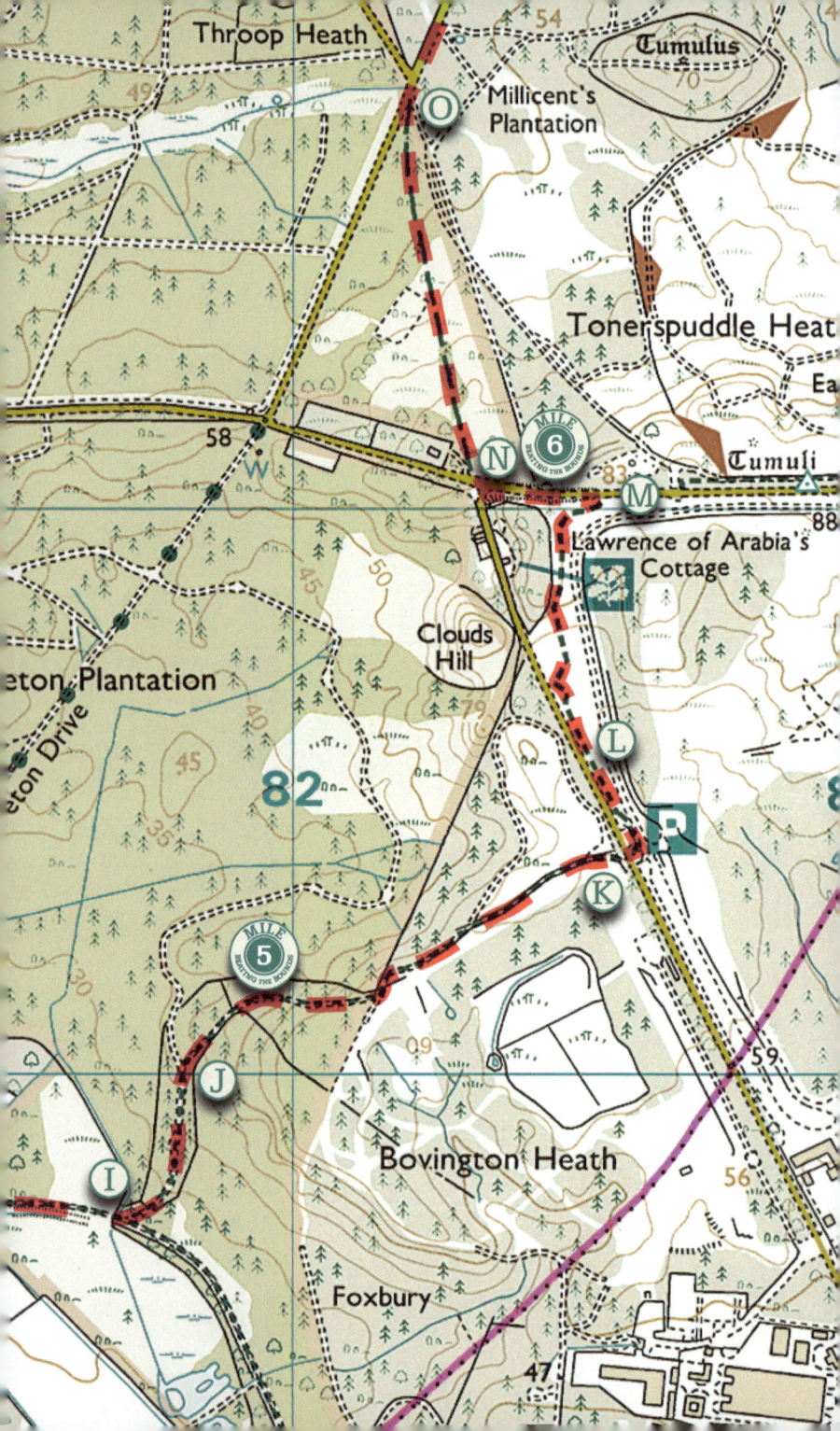

Thus instructed, proceed along the path bound by barbed wire and yellow-topped posts on both sides, the restriction compensated by the coconut scented gorse flowering profusely beyond the fence, and on a breezy day, you can also enjoy the distant oceanic roar of the wind in the pine-tops.

At the end of this path, pass through a green painted metal kissing gate onto the road to Bovington Ⓚ. Opposite is a lay-by with information boards giving details of the military vehicles sometimes to be seen on the tank training grounds, together with historical notes about Bovington Camp.

Look out for the continuation of the Lawrence Trail leading out of the left-hand end of the lay-by, and follow the path running parallel with the road. Shortly, to be seen on the left of the path, is a low standing stone Ⓛ marking the spot close to where T.E. Lawrence, known more universally as 'Lawrence of Arabia', was killed in a motorcycle accident in May 1935.

Continue along the pine needle-strewn path, curving to the right and slightly uphill to meet a road Ⓜ, and turn left to follow the grassy verge down to the junction with the road to Bovington on the left Ⓝ.

Another short detour is possible here to visit Clouds Hill, the home of T.E. Lawrence, now a National Trust property, where much more can be learnt about this enigmatic former resident of the parish.

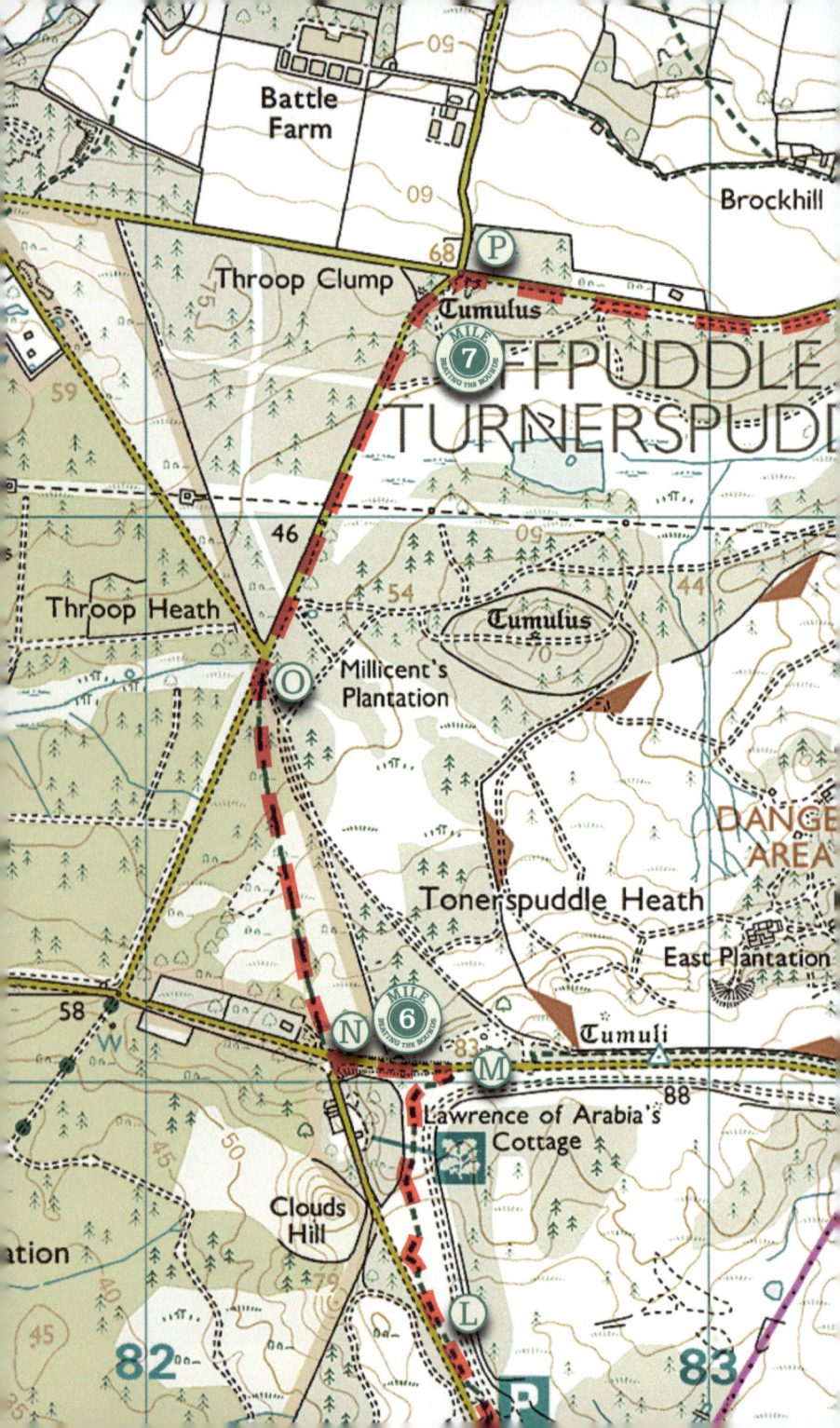

Returning again to Beating the Bounds, take the signed path directly opposite the junction with the Bovington road, the first few yards of which may be slightly overgrown, and go through a gate onto Turnerspuddle Heath.

Follow the narrow sandy path heading off to the left flanked by heather (more ankle tickling), and sizeable gorse bushes (seriously elbow scratching). Keep straight ahead, enjoying the profusion of yellow flower, eventually passing through a metal gate onto a road opposite a junction Ⓞ.

Turn right along the road, crossing a cattle grid, after which the road begins to rise, gradually at first and then more steeply, through trees up to the crossroads at Throop Clump Ⓟ.

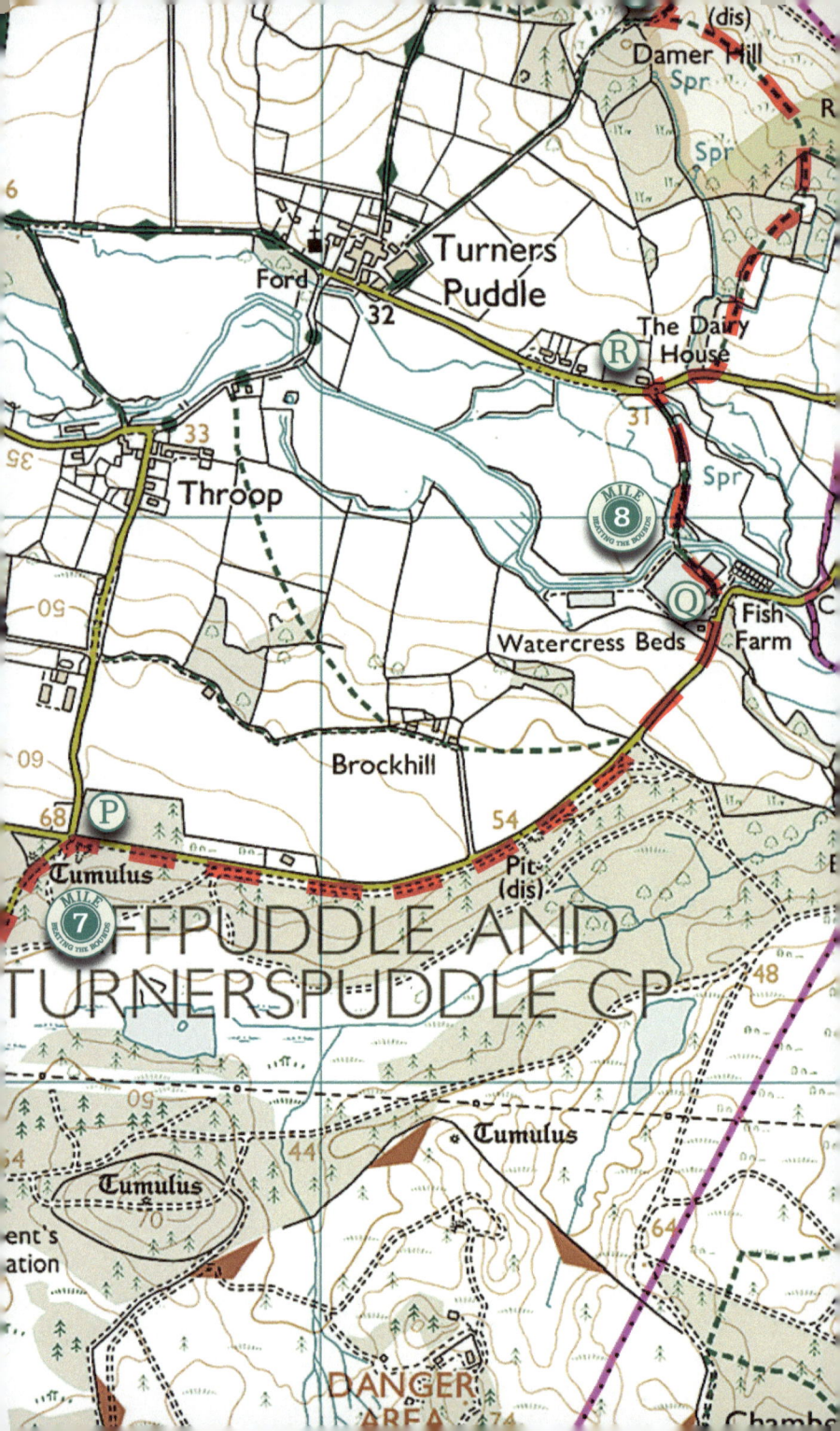

Turn right at the crossroads Ⓟ, following the sign to Turnerspuddle and Bere Regis, keeping to the edge of the military training area on the right. More attractive vistas appear on the left, as gaps between the trees reveal the Piddle Valley to the north.

The road curves to the left, descending gradually, and on reaching a watercress farm on the left Ⓠ, take the footpath signed to the left through a large gate topped with deer-proof netting, and walk along the concrete walkway between the watercress beds.

Watercress production, here in the parish, uses water from natural springs feeding the river. The water rises from deep in the chalk strata, at a constant 10°C all year round, and is exceptionally pure.

At the far end of the walkway, go through another gate in the deer fencing, being sure to close it securely behind you in the interests of maintaining the water purity.

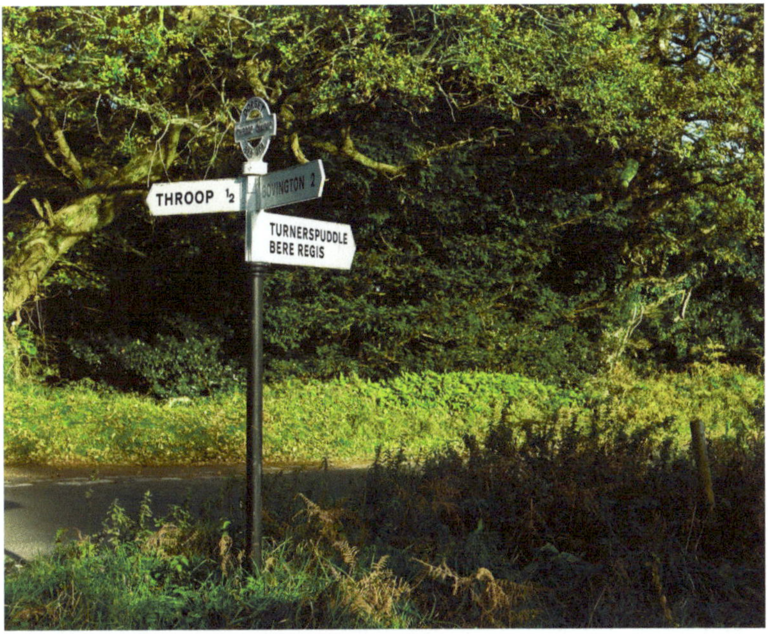

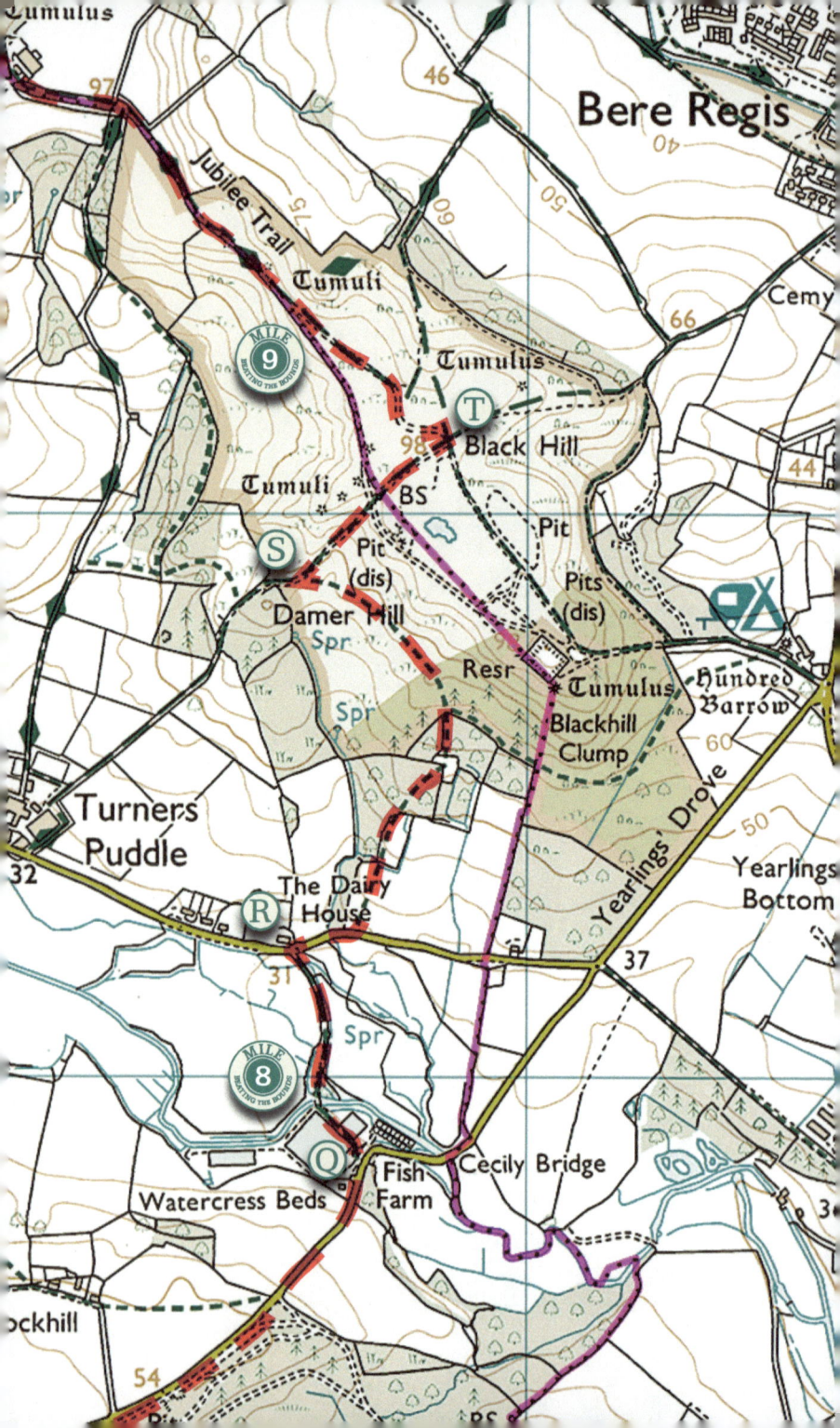

Cross a wooden bridge over the River Piddle, then after a few steps another bridge across a tributary stream, and continue along a rough track through the woods.

The permanently muddy section towards the end of this track can be bypassed using the sturdy wooden walkways, to emerge onto the road to Turnerspuddle, opposite The Dairy House Ⓡ.

Turn right, and at the next bend in the road after a short distance, take the signed footpath to the left up a bank into woodland. Follow the path as it winds its way gently uphill through this very attractive wood with a fine mix of trees, including holly, hazel, rowan, oak, ash and sycamore, all rising from a sea of bluebells in springtime, interspersed with wild euphorbia.

Passing through a metal kissing gate, the presence of bracken fronds and the sound once again of the wind in the pine-tops heralds a change back to more sandy, acidic soil and hence to heathland flora.

Continue through high gorse on either side, and at a T-junction with another path, turn left and follow the lower contour of Black Hill rising on the right, being careful not to trip on the many tree roots crisscrossing the path, until meeting another more substantial path at a T-junction by a large oak tree Ⓢ.

Turn right, and prepare for a steep but relatively short rise up a stony path to the ridge of Black Hill Ⓣ.

Ahead is a sarsen stone of the sort used to construct Stonehenge, although the one found here is on a somewhat smaller scale! It is known locally as the Devil's Stone and stands on the parish boundary.

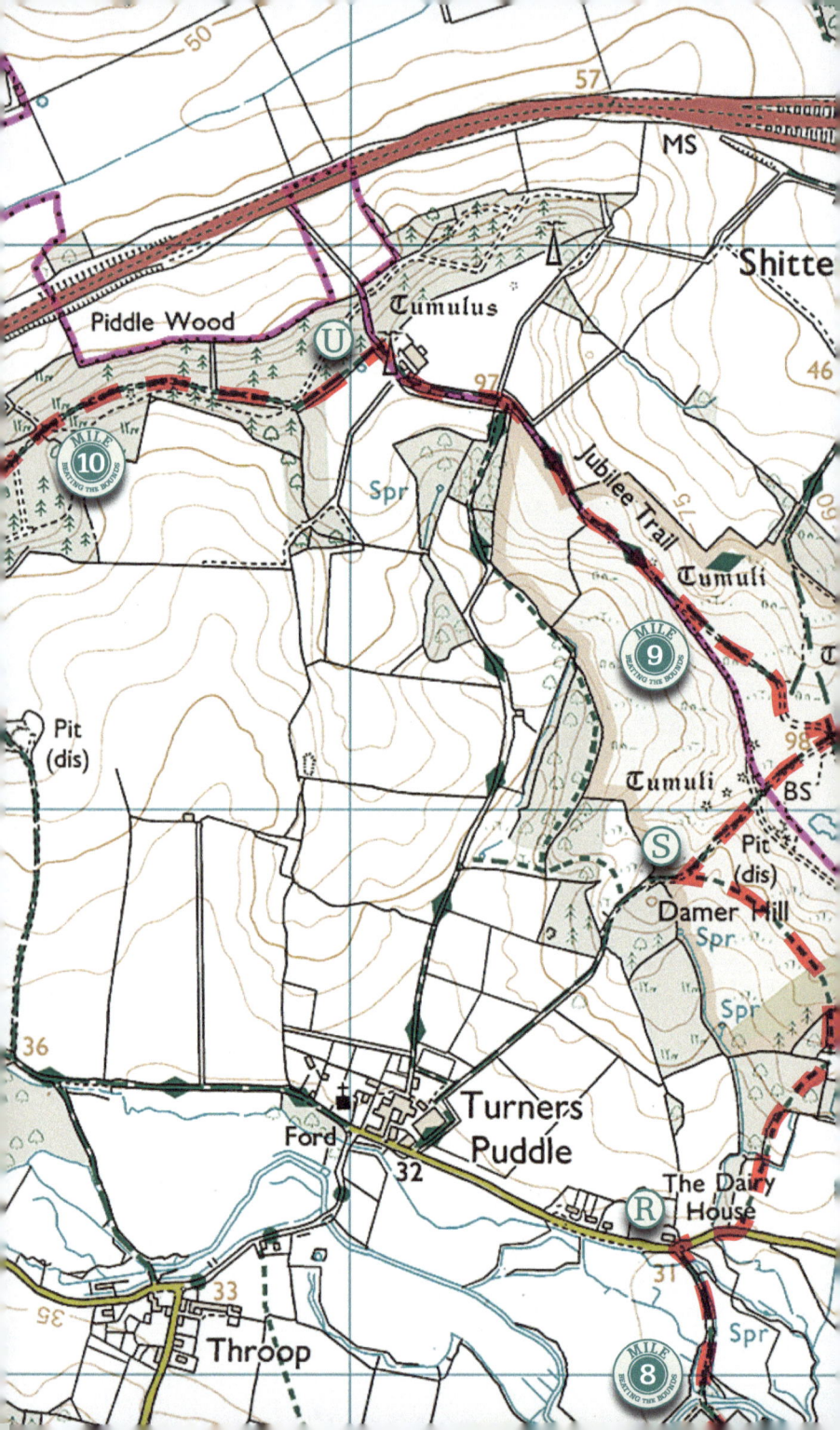

Turn left opposite the Devil's Stone and continue along the ridge-top path. Here there are fine views over the Piddle Valley to the south, and to the sweeping ridge ahead, magnificently purple-capped when the heather is in flower. This is part of the landscape that inspired Hardy's 'Egdon Heath'.

Unfortunately, part way along the ridge, dense gorse can engulf the path if not cut back, not only obscuring the views, but making the route ahead near impassable. If this is the case, rather than entering the gorse 'tunnel' it might be necessary to retrace your steps back to the Devil's Stone, turn left, and then after a short distance turn left again at a grassy crossroads to follow a track that will meet up with the far end of the gorse 'tunnel'.

Continue along the track, where now there are views over Bere Regis to the north. Pass through a gateway, and further ahead continue straight over a crossroads of tracks. Curve right skirting round some old farm buildings, and then take the bridleway signed to the left ⓤ, rising up a short bank, and then running between fences along the edge of a field under the boughs of a row of tall pines.

On reaching the edge of Piddle Wood ahead, keep to the main track through the trees, following the bridleway signs over a crossing of tracks. Continue through the trees, where there is some new planting with deer protection, and then along an undulating section which is slightly more open, before entering denser woodland again.

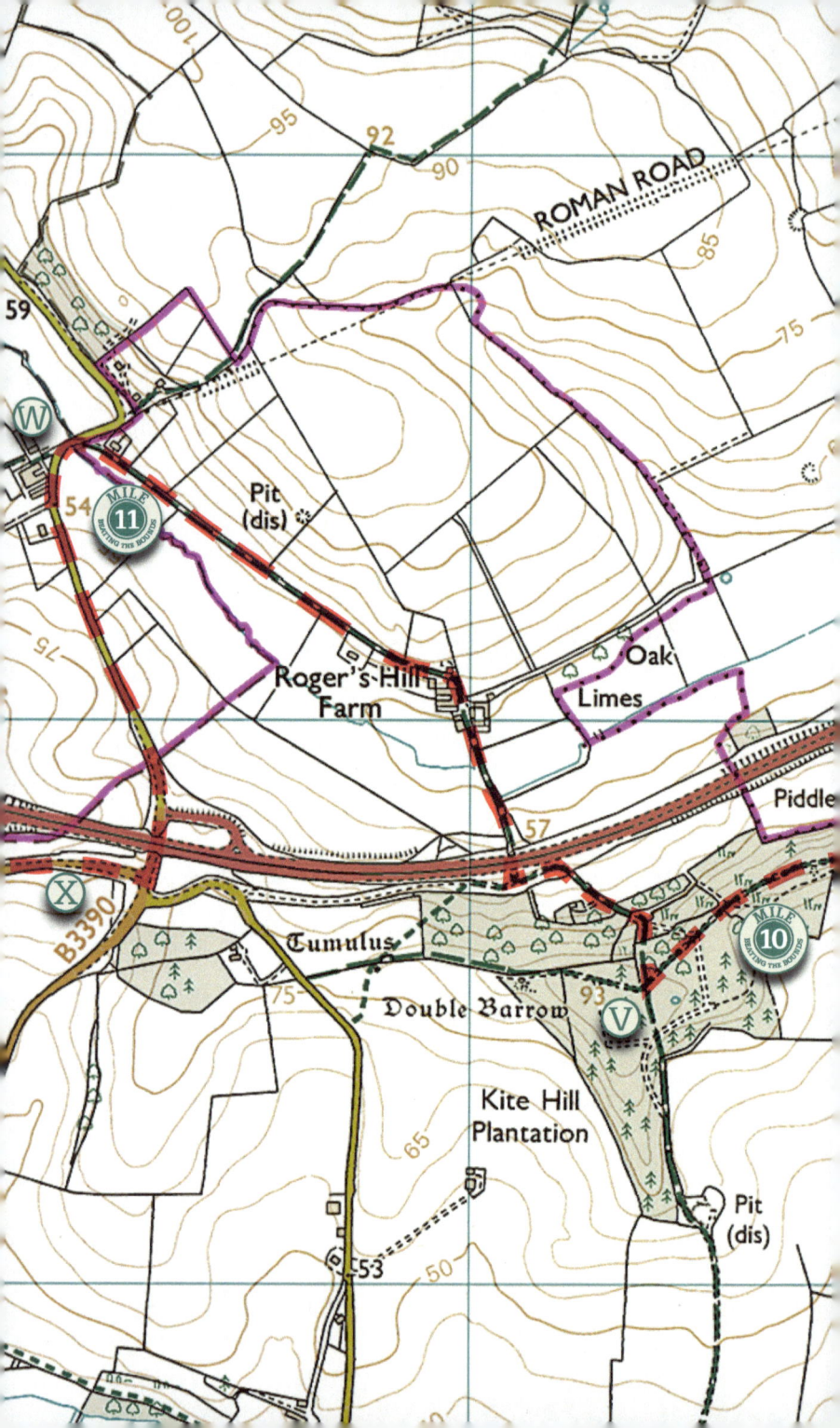

Coming to a wide crossing in the woods Ⓥ turn right onto a track that soon becomes a metalled lane leading fairly steeply downhill.

Pass through a gate and continue along the narrow lane towards the increasingly noisy A35.

Go right through the underpass beneath the main road and continue along the track towards Roger's Hill Farm.

Pass between farm buildings, bearing left along a straight, hedge-lined track eventually emerging on a minor road. Turn left to cross a stream Ⓦ, pausing for a moment on the bridge to consider that Roman soldiers once strode over this very spot as this short section of modern road follows the line of the Roman road running between Dorchester (Durnovaria) and Badbury Rings, with further Roman roads radiating from both these points.

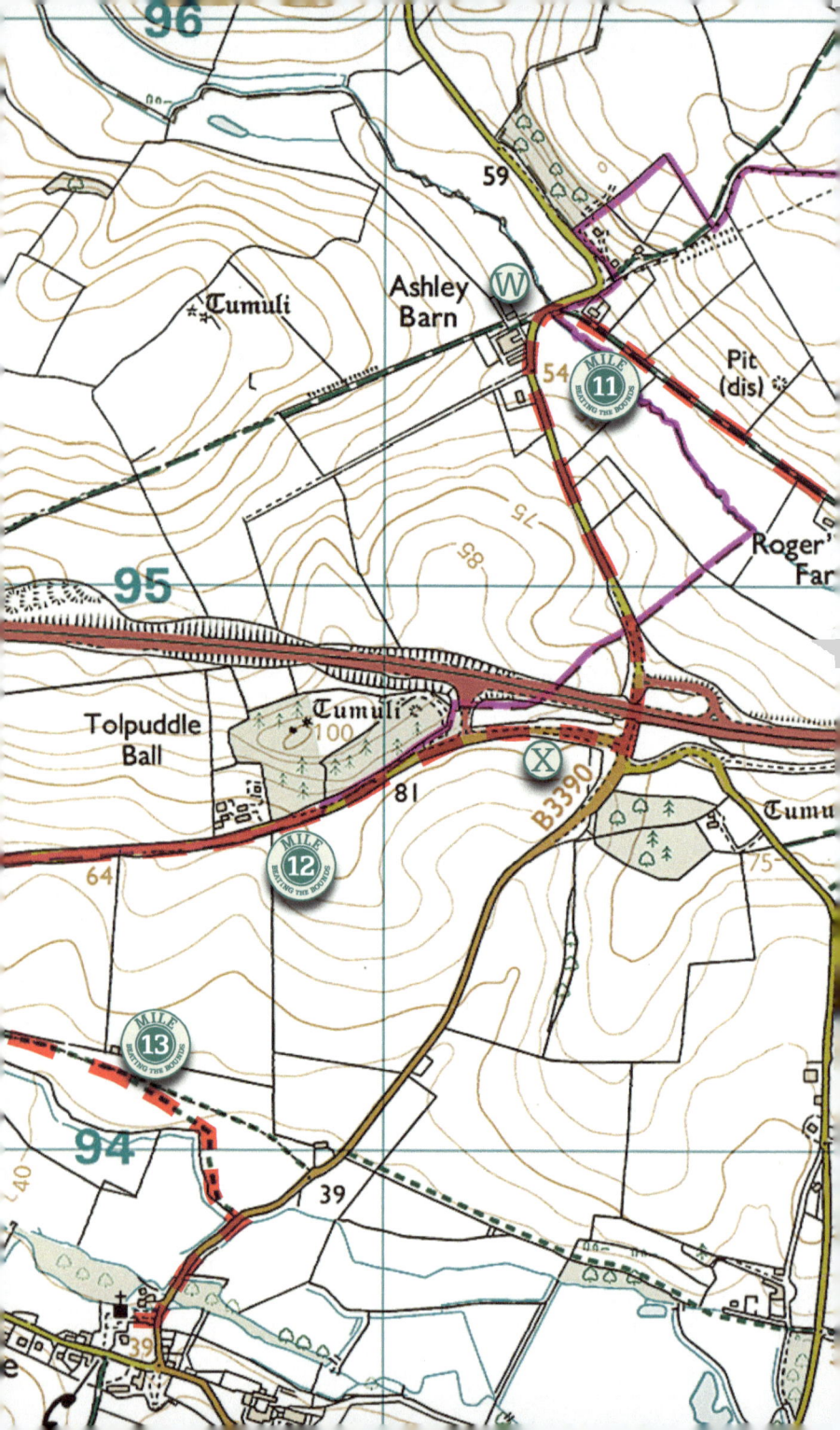

Continue along the road, curving left passing a large horse chestnut tree, resplendent with white candles in the spring, and then past farm buildings on the right, rising gradually between grassy banks towards the A35 once again.

Pass under the main road, and immediately turn right ⓧ towards the renowned village of Tolpuddle following the course of the old A35 as it was, prior to the construction of the bypass in 1999.

The noise of the nearby dual carriageway is a price to pay for being able to walk along the grassy verge of the old road with no more than village traffic giving walkers a wide berth (hopefully)!

Follow the road, gently descending towards Tolpuddle, with views across to Affpuddle to the south. At a point roughly halfway down the incline, look out for a milestone on the left-hand side, indicating the distance to Dorchester (8 miles) and to Wimborne and Poole (14 miles).

Milestones are emblematic of the turnpike era running from the 17th to 19th centuries when turnpike trusts were set up by individual Acts of Parliament with powers to collect tolls on principle roads.

In return, they were required to maintain those roads and to erect markers at one Statute mile intervals indicating the distance to towns along the road, helping to keep coaches to schedule.

At the height of the turnpike era, there were 20,000 miles of roads with milestones, but from the 1840s rail travel overtook road for longer journeys and turnpike trusts were wound up.

Many milestones were removed or defaced in World War II to baffle potential German invaders and many more have been demolished as roads have been widened, or have been smashed by hedge-cutters or flails, so this is a precious survivor!

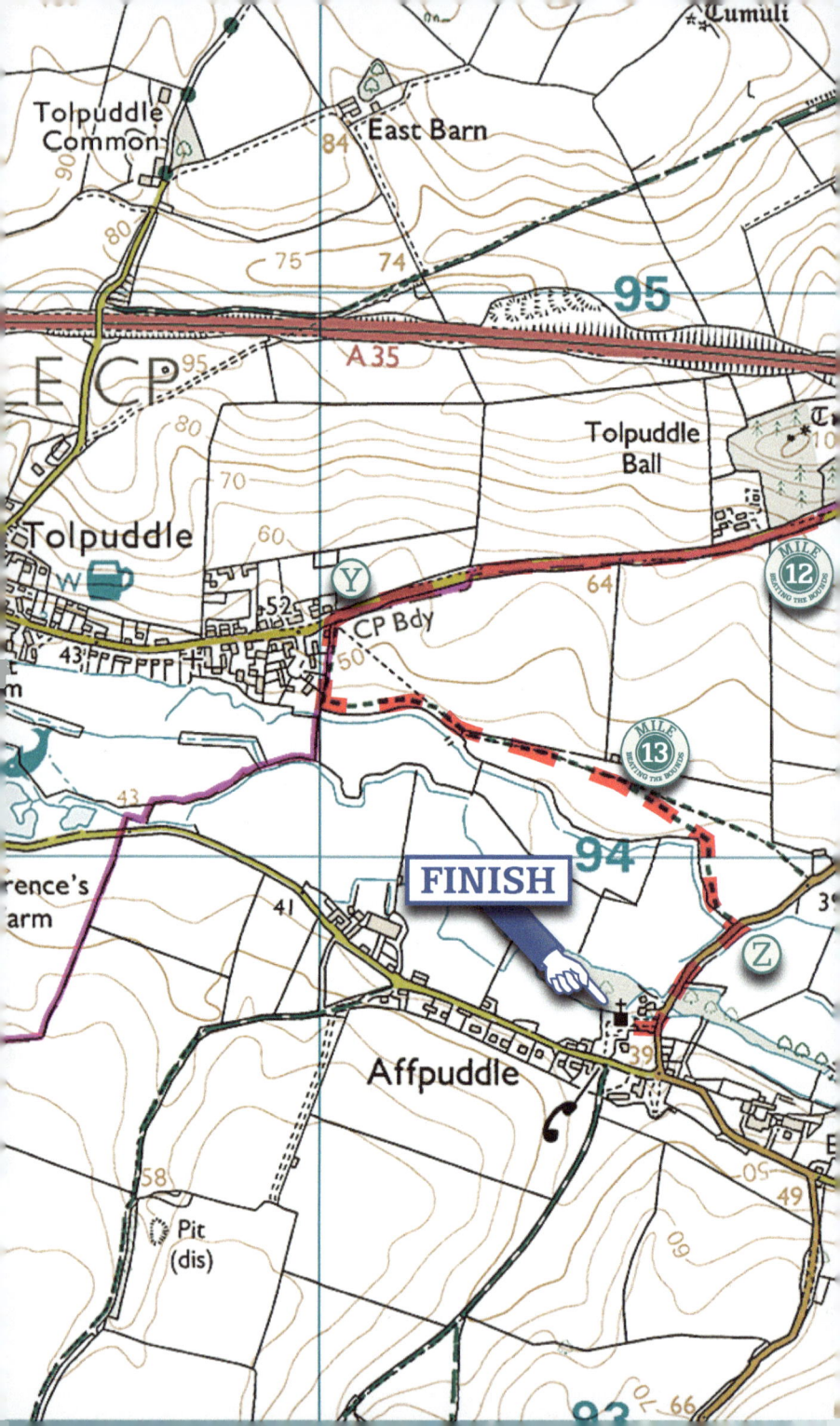

Immediately after the 30 mph sign at the entrance to Tolpuddle Ⓨ, take the footpath signed to Affpuddle on the left.

Keep to the right-hand edge of the field, which soon curves to the left, until reaching a stile next to a gate.

After climbing the stile, the next section of the path may be somewhat indistinct as it crosses through the middle of a field frequented by cattle. Keep a more or less central line, roughly parallel to the right-hand edge of the field, and after swinging towards the right, look out for a gap in the hedge ahead with a stile and footpath sign, leading onto the B3390 Ⓩ.

Turn right along the road, crossing the River Piddle once again, and when the tower of St Laurence's church appears on your right, clearly marking your destination, go through the gate into the Peace Garden, and then through the churchyard back to your starting point.

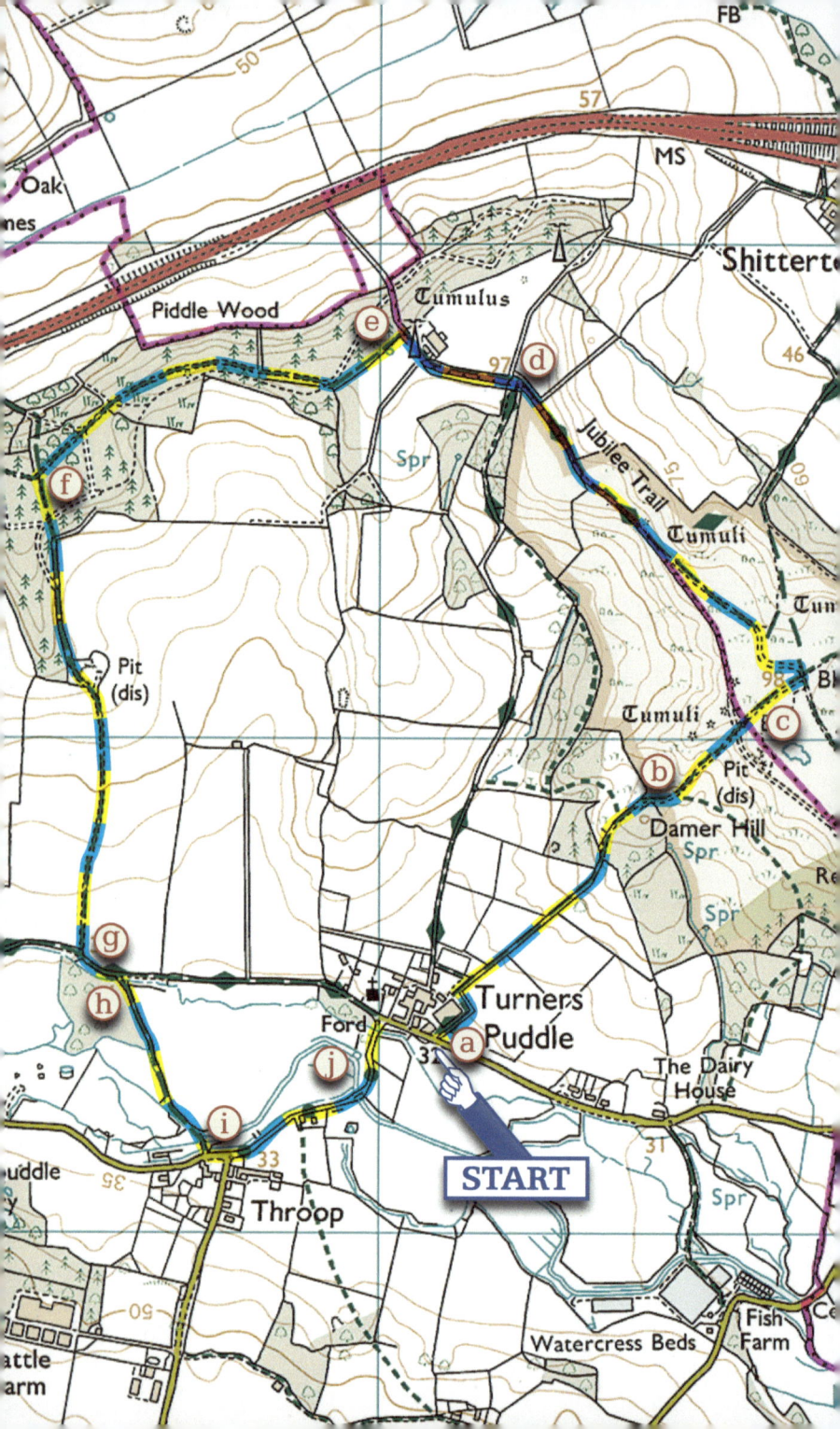

Circular Walk A

Turnerspuddle and Black Hill - 3⅓ miles

Park at the end of the no-through-road to Turnerspuddle, at the point where the metalled lane turns into a track just before the church of the Holy Trinity, now redundant following de-consecration in 1974.

Head back along the lane, and just after the farm buildings take the footpath on the left through a gate and then a metal 'squeezer' designed to deter motorcycles ⓐ.

The path swings left to skirt round the farm buildings, and then right to rise gradually between laid hedges. After a section with steep banks on either side (that can become rather muddy after rain), there is a metal gate after which the path flattens out and meanders through pleasant woodland.

Where a path joins from the right by a large oak tree, keep straight ahead ⓑ, now following the Beating the Bounds route.

Prepare for a steep but relatively short rise up a stony path to the ridge of Black Hill. Ahead is a sarsen stone of the sort used to construct Stonehenge, although the one found here is on a somewhat smaller scale! It is known locally as the Devil's Stone and stands on the parish boundary ⓒ.

Turn left opposite the Devil's Stone and continue along the ridge-top path. Here there are fine views over the Piddle Valley to the south, and to the sweeping ridge ahead, magnificently purple-capped when the heather is in flower. This is part of the landscape that inspired Hardy's 'Egdon Heath'.

Unfortunately, part way along the ridge, dense gorse can engulf the path if not cut back, not only obscuring the views, but making the route ahead near impassable. If this is the case, rather than entering the gorse 'tunnel' it might be necessary to retrace your steps back to the Devil's Stone, turn left, and then after a short distance turn left again at a grassy crossroads to follow a track that will meet up with the far end of the gorse 'tunnel'.

Continue along the track, where now there are views over Bere Regis to the north. Pass through a gateway, and further ahead continue straight over a crossroads of tracks ⓓ.

Curve right skirting round some old farm buildings, and then take the bridleway signed to the left ⓔ, rising up a short bank, and then running between fences along the edge of a field under the boughs of a row of tall pines.

On reaching the edge of Piddle Wood ahead, keep to the main track through the trees, following the bridleway signs over a crossing of tracks. Continue through the trees, where there is some new planting with deer protection, and then along an undulating section which is slightly more open, before entering denser woodland again.

Coming to a wide crossing in the woods turn left ⓕ and stay in the woods, soon swinging sharp right and then gently curving downhill through the tall conifers.

Emerging out of the conifers there are views across sweeping fields back to Black Hill, although the path stays rather enclosed before breaking through to the open by the entrance to an old chalk pit. Here there are fine views across the Piddle Valley to Briantspuddle as the path gradually descends between fields.

On reaching a track ⓖ, turn left towards Turnerspuddle, and then after a short distance turn right to follow a path signed to Throop ⓗ.

The path goes through woodland, soon running alongside a small stream leading to the wider River Piddle.

Follow the left bank of the swift-flowing river, then crossing it via a brick bridge where there is an attractive bench and rowan tree commemorating HM Queen Elizabeth II Diamond Jubilee in 2012 ⓘ.

Turn left on the road ahead, and then where the road bears right, continue straight ahead along the track signed as a no-through-road. The track heads back towards the River Piddle, which it fords, although a sturdy footbridge can be used next to the ford ⓘ.

The track continues on towards Turnerspuddle, finally crossing a smaller ford, again with the option of a footbridge, to return to the parking area near the church.

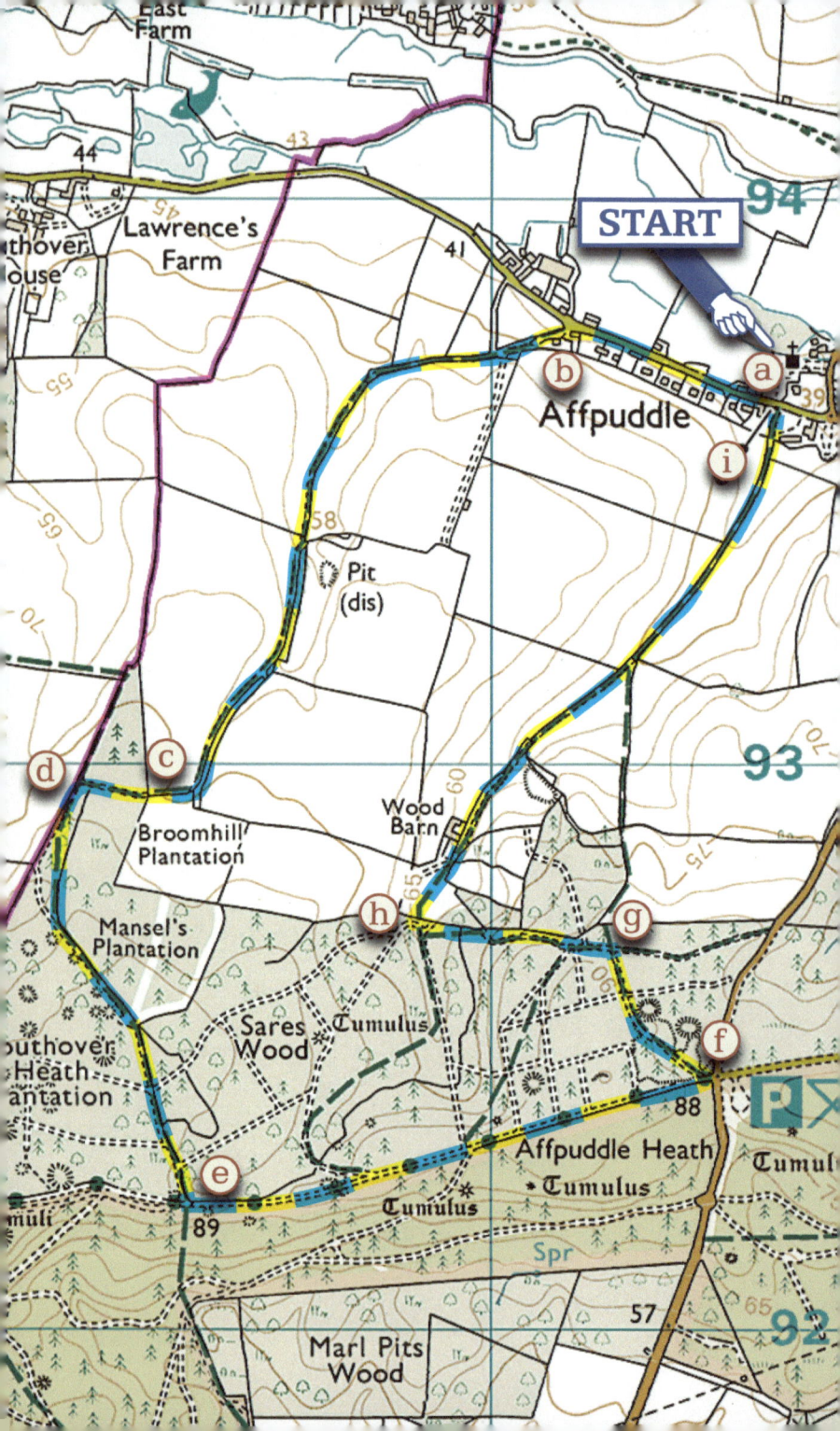

Circular Walk B

Affpuddle and Sares Wood - 3⅓ miles

Park by the church of St. Laurence ⓐ, the same starting point as the Beating the Bounds walk, where there is room enough for a few cars to park alongside the churchyard.

This fine church, which is open daily, dates originally from the 13th century, enlarged later in the 15th century with an aisle and a splendid tower in the Perpendicular style. Inside are interesting pew ends, some with poppy head finials. The pulpit has five panels containing finely carved figures below which are medallions with the symbols of the Four Evangelists and the fifth of the pelican (which, according to legend, would pierce its own chest in order to feed blood to its young).

Head west along the road through the village, and then where the road bears slightly right ⓑ, take the bridleway on the left, initially a metalled track, leading up a slight incline.

Ignoring tracks to the left and right, continue along the bridleway between hedges and then curving left to skirt the edge of first one large field, and then a second, eventually reaching a gate by a large oak tree in front of a dark conifer wood ⓒ.

Passing through the gate, follow the path through the towering conifers. This section may be rutted and muddy in wet weather, but after a short distance the path meets another at right angles ⓓ, and turning left the new path should be firmer underfoot. The woodland now becomes slightly more open, with oak and beech mixed in, and in springtime bluebells line the path.

Keep to the main track, ignoring any forestry tracks to left or right, eventually passing to the side of a metal vehicle barrier to emerge onto a substantial track, the Hardy Way ⓔ.

Turn left and follow the Hardy Way, which remains a wide track with a good mix of deciduous and evergreen trees on either side, until reaching the B3390 ⓕ.

Go through a wooden gate to the side of a metal vehicle barrier, and turn sharp left beside another barrier to take a path leading away from the road through tall conifers.

Continue straight ahead, passing some tree-filled sinkholes to the right, and on reaching a crossing of paths, turn left ⓖ.

Keep straight ahead, ignoring other paths leading off to the left, as the path emerges out of the conifers and then descends at first gradually, and considerably more steeply into mixed leaved woodland with beech, oak and sweet chestnut interspersed amongst the conifers, and a deep carpet of moss covering fallen trunks and branches.

On reaching the bottom of the small v-shaped valley in the woods, turn right ⓗ and go through a metal gate out of the woods, and keep straight ahead towards a barn and farm storage area. Skirt to the right of this, following the track between fields with just a wire fence on the left at first, then becoming more enclosed by hedges and banks on either side as it gently descends back towards Affpuddle.

Where the track meets the road opposite the church, there is a red telephone box on the left-hand side ⓘ – a 'classic' K6 type. The 'Kiosk No. 6' was the first red telephone box to be used extensively outside London, and was designed to commemorate the Silver Jubilee of King George V in 1935, and consequently sometimes known as the 'Jubilee' kiosk.

It no longer contains a telephone. With the demise of public pay phone use, it has been converted to house a defibrillator.

Circular Walk C

Clouds Hill and Moreton Drive - 3 miles

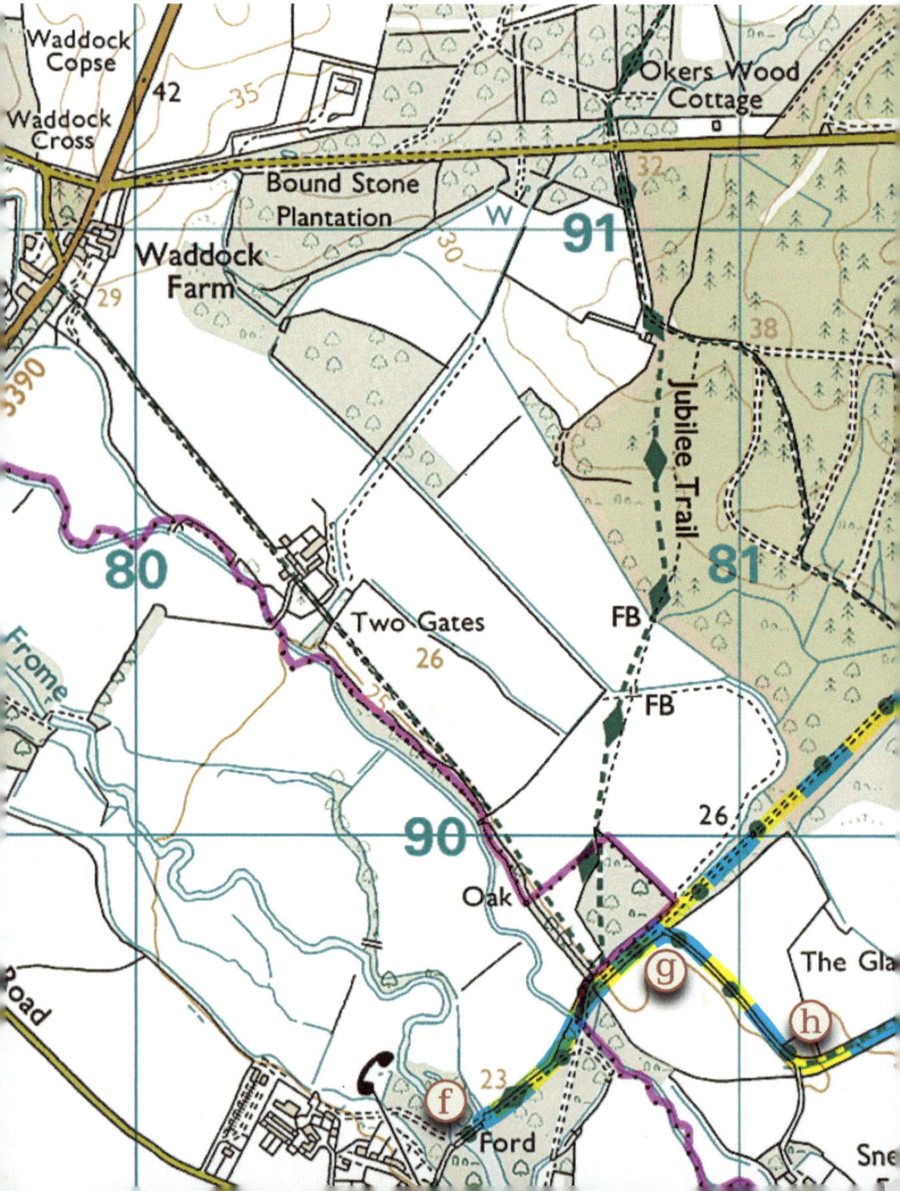

Park in the lay-by on the road between Clouds Hill and Bovington ⓐ. The lay-by has information boards giving details of the military vehicles sometimes to be seen on the tank training grounds, together with historical notes about Bovington Camp.

Look out for a sign indicating the Lawrence Trail leading out of the left-hand end of the lay-by, and follow the path running parallel with the road. Shortly, to be seen on the left of the path, is a low standing stone ⓑ marking the spot close to where T.E. Lawrence,

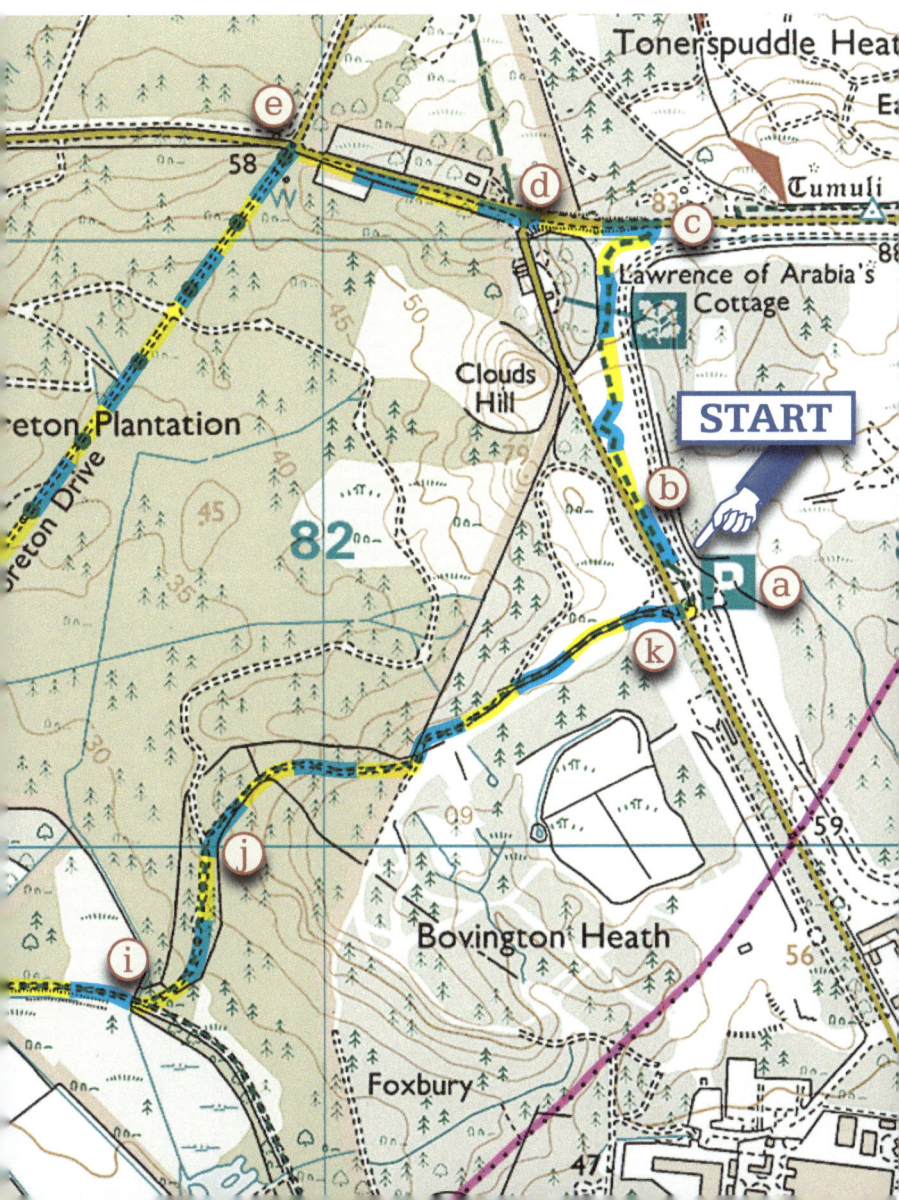

known more universally as 'Lawrence of Arabia', was killed in a motorcycle accident in May 1935.

Continue along the pine needle-strewn path, curving to the right and slightly uphill to meet a road ⓒ, and turn left to follow the grassy verge down to the junction with the road to Bovington on the left ⓓ. Another short detour is possible here to visit Clouds Hill, the home of T.E. Lawrence, now a National Trust property, where much more can be learnt about this enigmatic former resident of the parish.

Continue straight along the road until reaching a junction on the right ⓔ. Opposite the junction on the left is a wide track which is the start of Moreton Drive. Follow this track, heading gradually downhill in a straight line through Moreton Plantation. The conifer planting is not dense here, so the track is fairly open and well used by walkers and cyclists.

Although the route does not cross the River Frome, it is worth following Moreton Drive all the way to a long, low footbridge and ford across a wide, shallow section of the river ⓕ, a popular spot for children in the summer months.

Rather than crossing the ford, retrace your steps for a short distance back up Moreton Drive, and then turn right ⓖ along a track signed as the Lawrence Trail, rejoining the Beating the Bounds route.

Pass to the left of a dying oak tree (with just two small branches valiantly clinging to life at the time of writing), and then swing to the left ⓗ and continue through a pleasant section of mixed woodland. Pass a ruined house on the left and go through a wooden gate, after which the trees begin to thin until the path emerges into a Savanna-like grassland area.

At a junction of tracks by a group of young oaks ⓘ, turn left keeping to the signed Lawrence Trail, and follow the sandy path flanked at first by bracken and gorse, and then by conifers.

A little way ahead, leave the main track, turning right onto a path opposite another Lawrence Trail waymark ⓙ.

Head uphill, keeping to the stony path, until reaching a metal kissing gate in the fence marking the edge of the military training area. There is a sign indicating that your enjoyment of the walk depends on, amongst other things, NOT touching ANY suspicious objects, and keeping to the footpath designated by the yellow-topped posts at all times.

Thus instructed, proceed along the path bound by barbed wire and yellow-topped posts on both sides, the restriction compensated by the coconut scented gorse flowering profusely beyond the fence, and on a breezy day, you can also enjoy the distant oceanic roar of the wind in the pine-tops.

At the end of this path, pass through a green painted metal kissing gate onto the road to Bovington (k) and cross over to the lay-by to return to the starting point.

The Countryside Code

© Crown Copyright

Respect other people

Please respect the local community and other people using the outdoors. Remember your actions can affect people's lives and livelihoods.

Consider the local community and other people enjoying the outdoors

Respect the needs of local people and visitors alike – for example, don't block gateways, driveways or other paths with your vehicle.

When riding a bike or driving a vehicle, slow down or stop for horses, walkers and farm animals and give them plenty of room. By law, cyclists must give way to walkers and horse-riders on bridleways.

Co-operate with people at work in the countryside. For example, keep out of the way when farm animals are being gathered or moved and follow directions from the farmer.

Busy traffic on small country roads can be unpleasant and dangerous to local people, visitors and wildlife - so slow down and where possible, leave your vehicle at home, consider sharing lifts and use alternatives such as public transport or cycling.

Leave gates and property as you find them and follow paths unless wider access is available

A farmer will normally close gates to keep farm animals in, but may sometimes leave them open so the animals can reach food and water. Leave gates as you find them or follow instructions on signs. When in a group, make sure the last person knows how to leave the gates.

Follow paths unless wider access is available, such as on open country or registered common land (known as 'open access' land).

If you think a sign is illegal or misleading such as a 'Private - No Entry' sign on a public path, contact the local authority.

Leave machinery and farm animals alone – don't interfere with animals even if you think they're in distress. Try to alert the farmer instead.

Use gates, stiles or gaps in field boundaries if you can – climbing over walls, hedges and fences can damage them and increase the risk of farm animals escaping.

Our heritage matters to all of us – be careful not to disturb ruins and historic sites.

Protect the natural environment

We all have a responsibility to protect the countryside now and for future generations, so make sure you don't harm animals, birds, plants or trees and try to leave no trace of your visit.

When out with your dog make sure it is not a danger or nuisance to farm animals, horses, wildlife or other people.

Leave no trace of your visit and take your litter home

Protecting the natural environment means taking special care not to damage, destroy or remove features such as rocks, plants and trees. They provide homes and food for wildlife, and add to everybody's enjoyment of the countryside.

Litter and leftover food doesn't just spoil the beauty of the countryside, it can be dangerous to wildlife and farm animals – so take your litter home with you. Dropping litter and dumping rubbish are criminal offences.

Fires can be as devastating to wildlife and habitats as they are to people and property – so be careful with naked flames and cigarettes at any time of the year. Sometimes, controlled fires are used to manage vegetation, particularly on heaths and moors between 1 October and 15 April, but if a fire appears to be unattended then report it by calling 999.

Keep dogs under effective control

When you take your dog into the outdoors, always ensure it does not disturb wildlife, farm animals, horses or other people by keeping it under effective control.

This means that you:

- keep your dog on a lead, or
- keep it in sight at all times, be aware of what it's doing and be confident it will return to you promptly on command
- ensure it does not stray off the path or area where you have a right of access

Special dog rules may apply in particular situations, so always look out for local signs – for example:

- dogs may be banned from certain areas that people use, or there may be restrictions, byelaws or control orders limiting where they can go
- the access rights that normally apply to open country and registered common land (known as 'open access' land) require dogs to be kept on a short lead between 1 March and 31 July, to help protect ground nesting birds, and all year round near farm animals

- at the coast, there may also be some local restrictions to require dogs to be kept on a short lead during the bird breeding season, and to prevent disturbance to flocks of resting and feeding birds during other times of year

It's always good practice (and a legal requirement on 'open access' land) to keep your dog on a lead around farm animals and horses, for your own safety and for the welfare of the animals. A farmer may shoot a dog which is attacking or chasing farm animals without being liable to compensate the dog's owner.

However, if cattle or horses chase you and your dog, it is safer to let your dog off the lead – don't risk getting hurt by trying to protect it. Your dog will be much safer if you let it run away from a farm animal in these circumstances and so will you.

Everyone knows how unpleasant dog mess is and it can cause infections, so always clean up after your dog and get rid of the mess responsibly – 'bag it and bin it'. Make sure your dog is wormed regularly to protect it, other animals and people.

Enjoy the outdoors

Even when going out locally, it's best to get the latest information about where and when you can go. For example, your rights to go onto some areas of open access land and coastal land may be restricted in particular places at particular times. Find out as much as you can about where you are going, plan ahead and follow advice and local signs.

Plan ahead and be prepared

You'll get more from your visit if you refer to up-to-date maps or guidebooks and websites before you go. Visit Natural England on GOV.UK or contact local information centres or libraries for a list of outdoor recreation groups offering advice on specialist activities.

You're responsible for your own safety and for others in your care – especially children - so be prepared for natural hazards, changes in weather and other events.

Wild animals, farm animals and horses can behave unpredictably if you get too close, especially if they're with their young - so give them plenty of space.

Check weather forecasts before you leave. Conditions can change rapidly especially on mountains and along the coast, so don't be afraid to turn back.

Part of the appeal of the countryside is that you can get away from it all. You may not see anyone for hours, and there are many places without clear mobile phone signals, so let someone else know where you're going and when you expect to return.

Follow advice and local signs

England has about 190,000 km (118,000 miles) of public rights of way, providing many opportunities to enjoy the natural environment. Get to know the signs and symbols used in the countryside to show paths and open countryside. See the Countryside Code leaflet for some of the symbols you may come across.

Information

For further information about the parish, its history, landscape and wildlife, visit our information kiosk at the crossroads in Briantspuddle.

www.ingramcontent.com/pod-product-compliance
Lightning Source LLC
Chambersburg PA
CBHW041228070526
44584CB00006B/328